THE JADE FLUTE

CHINESE POEMS IN PROSE

PETER PAUPER PRESS
MOUNT VERNON
NEW YORK

THE JADE FLUTE

• • •

CHINESE
POEMS
IN
PROSE

CONTENTMENT

WHEN YOU ASK WHY I DWELL HERE DOCILE AMONG THE FAR GREEN HILLS, I LAUGH IN MY HEART. MY HEART IS HAPPY.

THE PEACH-BLOSSOM WATCHES THE RIVER RUNNING BUT REMAINS CONTENT. THERE IS A BETTER HEAVEN AND EARTH THAN THE BUSY WORLD OF MEN. [*Li Po*]

• • •

I HAVE SEEN A ROAD

I HAVE SEEN A ROAD THAT WANDERS IN GREEN SHADE, THAT RUNS THROUGH SWEET FIELDS OF FLOWERS. MY EYES HAVE TRAVELED THERE, AND JOURNEYED FAR ALONG THAT COOL FINE ROAD.

BUT I WILL NEVER REALLY WALK THAT ROAD; IT DOES NOT REALLY LEAD TO WHERE SHE LIVES.

WHEN SHE WAS BORN, THEY BOUND HER LITTLE FEET WITH LEATHER BANDS; MY BELOVÈD NEVER WALKS THE ROAD OF SHADE AND FLOWERS.

WHEN SHE WAS BORN, THEY BOUND HER LITTLE HEART WITH LEATHER BANDS; MY BELOVÈD NEVER LISTENS TO MY SONG. [*Anonymous*]

FLOATING NARCISSUS

FADED NARCISSUS, FLOATING DOWN THE RIVER TO TIENOUAN . . . IF YOU SEE THERE A YOUNG GIRL DREAMING, UNDER A CINNAMON TREE THAT HAS BLOSSOMED TWICE SINCE WE EMBRACED, TELL HER . . . I SMELL A FRESH CARNATION TO REMEMBER HER PERFUME. [*Wan Ts'u*]

• • •

THE FRIENDS

YOU RODE A YELLOW HORSE, I RODE A WHITE ONE . . . HORSES TWO COLORS, BUT OUR BOYISH HEARTS WERE ONE.

WE RODE TOGETHER THROUGH THE COUNTRY, A PAIR OF PRANCING PEACOCKS . . . OUR JEWELED LONG SWORDS SHINING IN THE SUN, OUR TALL HEADDRESSES SCARLET, AND OUR PRECIOUS FURS WORTH THOUSANDS . . . WE WERE GUESTS OF ALL FIVE ORDERS OF NOBILITY.

NOW, MY FIERCE TIGER FRIEND HAS CRASHED INTO A TRAP. IT IS FINE TO FACE FATE NOBLY . . . BUT IF MY BRAVE COMRADE IS IN DANGER, WHAT PLEASURE CAN I FIND IN BEING FREE AND HAPPY?

[*Li Po*]

A NEGLECTED WIFE

A WINDOW OPENS AND A BEAUTIFUL WOMAN LOOKS OUT. HER EYES ARE WET AS SHE LOOKS AT GRASS TURNING GREEN BEFORE HER HOUSE, AT WILLOWS IN NEW LEAF ALONG THE RIVER. IN TIMES PAST, WHEN SHE LOOKED OUT, SHE SANG.

WHEN YOU OWN A TREASURE YOU MUST KNOW HOW TO KEEP IT. MY FRIEND, YOURS HAS TWO BEAUTIFUL LEGS: BE CAREFUL, OR IT WILL RUN AWAY!

[*Mei Chang*]

• • •

THE POET AND THE DANCERS

HERE, DAY AND NIGHT, THE PRETTIEST WOMEN OF THE EMPIRE ARE DANCING . . . SONGS AND LAUGHTER ECHO FROM THE GOLDEN SCREENS.

WHEN ALL THE OTHERS ARE OVERCOME WITH DRINKING, I PUT DOWN MY WINE. I TAKE MY BRUSH, I WET THE GOLDEN INK, AND I WRITE SAD POEMS WITH SWAYING CHARACTERS THAT LOOK LIKE THESE ROSY BODIES STREWN ON A MARBLE FLOOR.

[*Chang Wu-chien*]

I WILL BE ALONE

THIS LAKE AT KUEN-MING, HOW WONDROUS IT WAS IN THE DAYS OF HAN! THEN IT FLOATED A PARADE OF PROUD WAR-JUNKS GAY WITH FLAGS . . . NOW IT IS ONLY A BARE MIRROR AT NIGHT FOR THE SPINNING BOY . . . THAT STAR-BOY WHO DOES NOT FLEE FROM COLD.

BLACK SEED-PODS FROM THE KOUMI BLOW ON IT NOW. THERE ARE LILIES AND LOTUS-FLOWERS TOO . . . BUT SOON THE NORTH WIND WILL RIP AWAY THEIR LEAVES.

AND I WILL BE ALONE WITH MY UNHAPPINESS.

[*Tu Fu*]

• • •

REMEMBER TO WEAR THEM

A SHADOW ON THE WINDOW-SCREEN . . . WHO COMES GATHERING MY FLOWERS? SHE MAY PICK THEM IF SHE WILL, BUT WHAT WILL SHE DO WITH THEM?

THE BEST SPRAYS ARE THERE BENEATH THE EAVES. PICK MORE OF THESE . . . AND REMEMBER, YOU WHO GATHER FLOWERS, WEAR THEM IN YOUR HAIR.

[*Chiang Chieh*]

WILD GEESE

FAR IN THE NORTHWEST STANDS A HOUSE, HIGH ITS TOWER IN THE CLOUDS. EMBROIDERED CURTAINS ARE AT THE WINDOWS. THE TOWER RISES IN THREE STEPS, AND FROM THE TOWER FLOATS A SONG, A SAD SONG WITH A SAD LUTE PLAYING BESIDE IT. WHO CAN THE SINGER BE?

SURELY IT IS SHE WHO HAS NO HUSBAND LEFT TO HER, NO FATHER LEFT, NO CHILD. HER SONG FOLLOWS THE WIND; IT RISES AND FALLS. WITH THE SINGING, SOBBING. . . . GRIEF IS VICTOR OVER HER STRONG WILL.

SHE DOES NOT SORROW THAT HER LIFE IS SAD, BUT THAT SO FEW CAN UNDERSTAND THE SORROW IN HER SONG. O, TO FLY LIKE THOSE TWO WILD GEESE, RISING WITH BEATING WINGS!

[*Anonymous*]

• • •

CONTENTMENT

LAZILY WAVING A WHITE-FEATHERED FAN I LIE NAKED . . . A GREEN DELL IN THE MOUNTAINS. I HANG MY HAT ON A JUTTING ROCK . . . I COOL MY HEAD WITH PINEY AIR.

[*Li Po*]

TO THE EMPEROR

WITH THIS I SEND A MIRROR . . . IT IS PURE ROUND AND IT IS CLEAR WHITE, TO REMIND YOU OF THE MOON WE GAZED AT WHEN WE WERE LAST TOGETHER IN THE GARDEN.

MAY IT ALWAYS STAY WITH YOU, AND MAY IT STIR SWEET MEMORIES.

BUT I KNOW: BY AUTUMN YOU WILL CAST IT ASIDE FOR SOMETHING NEW, AS YOU HAVE CAST ASIDE ITS LOVING SENDER.

[*The emperor's favorite, Pan Tie tsu*]

● ● ●

WHEN THE SWALLOWS RETURNED

WHEN THE SWALLOWS RETURNED LAST YEAR THEY MADE THEIR NEST IN THE EMBROIDERY ROOM. THEY GATHERED CLAY FROM THE FLOWER-GARDEN, AND SCATTERED DUST OVER HARP AND BOOKS.

WHEN THE SWALLOWS RETURNED THIS YEAR, NO ONE HEARD THEIR TWITTERING SPEECH. SHE WHO HAD ROLLED UP THE SCREEN FOR THEM WAS THERE NO MORE. . . . IN THE AMBER TWILIGHT A SOFT-PATTERING RAIN. [*Hsin Ch'i-chi*]

THE WORLD AROUND US

DREAD LORD, DO NOT WAVE YOUR SCEPTER: IT IS BEJEWELED. DEAR DANCER, DO NOT WHIRL YOUR SCARVES: THEY ARE ORCHID-FLOWERED. PALE POET, DO NOT FLAUNT YOUR HEART: IT IS RADIANT WITH LOVE.

OUR WORLD CARES ONLY FOR UNENCHANTED THINGS. [*Li Po*]

• • •

YOUNG GIRLS OF OLD

IN A TINY GROVE WITH FLOWERS EVERYWHERE, YOUNG GIRLS OF DAYS GONE BY SIT LOOKING IN THEIR MIRRORS.

THEY SAY: "SOMETIMES WE THINK THAT WE HAVE GROWN OLD, THAT OUR HAIR IS WHITE AND OUR EYES NO LONGER CLEAR AS THE NEW MOON . . . BUT IT IS NOT TRUE! OUR MIRRORS ARE BEWITCHED WITH WINTER, AND THEY LIE! IT IS THE MIRRORS THAT MAKE OUR HAIR LIKE SNOW AND WRINKLE OUR YOUNG FACES! BUT WICKED WINTER CAN BEWITCH OUR MIRRORS ONLY, NOT OURSELVES . . . FOREVER, WE ARE UNCHANGED."

[*Wang Chang-ling*]

THE MINIATURE PAVILION

HERE IS THE LITTLE LAKE, HERE THE LITTLE PAVILION OF WHITE PORCELAIN. THE TINY JADE BRIDGE CURVES . . . THE BACK OF A CROUCHING LION.

BOON COMPANIONS GATHER IN THE MINIATURE HALL. THEY CHATTER AND DRINK WINE...THEY STARE AT THE FLICKERING REFLECTIONS OF PEONIES THAT LINE THE BANK. SOME OF THE COMPANIONS, LONG SLEEVES PUSHED BACK, CAPS LOW OVER EYES, ARE WRITING POEMS.

THE ARCH OF THE BRIDGE IS A CRESCENT MOON . . . THE REFLECTED PEONIES A COMPANY OF DANCING GIRLS [*Li Po*]

● ● ●

PICKING THE LOTUS

THE HARVEST MOON IS BURNING ON THE WATERS OF SOUTH LAKE. DRIFTING ALONE, I LEAN DOWN TO PICK WHITE LOTUS LILIES.

FIERCE DESIRE PULLS ME . . . I YEARN TO TELL THEM OF MY PASSION. ALAS, MY BOAT FLOATS AWAY AT MERCY OF THE MOVING CURRENT. MY HEART LOOKS BACK IN SADNESS. ✓ [*Li Po*]

THE ASHES OF MY HOUSE

WHEN I RETURNED TO THE HOUSE WHERE I HAD BEEN A HAPPY CHILD . . . ONLY A PILE OF ASHES WHERE IT HAD STOOD.

I WEPT LONG, AND TO FORGET MY WEEPING, I SAILED OUT ON THE VAST CALM SEA. ON THESE WATERS, IN A STAR-SAPPHIRE NIGHT, I PLAYED MY FLUTE TO THE SUMMER MOON . . . MY GRIEF MY MELODY. BUT THE MOON, A WOMAN'S FACE, SOON VEILED ITSELF WITH CLOUD.

I SAILED BACK TO SHORE, I WALKED AWAY FROM THE WATERS TO THE FRIENDLY FOREST . . . BUT THERE THE TREES TOO TURNED AWAY FROM ME. I KNEW THEN HAPPINESS WAS BURIED FOREVER UNDER A PILE OF ASHES.

RUNNING BACK TO THE SEA, I DECIDED TO DROWN MYSELF. BUT A WHITE BOAT SAILED ALONG THE SHORE. A YOUNG GIRL WAS SAILING IT.

O YOU WHO SMILED AT ME THAT DAY WHEN I WAS SUFFERING, O YOU WHO RESCUED ME FROM GRIEF . . . I WILL BUILD AGAIN THE HAPPY HOUSE OF MY CHILDHOOD, IN YOUR HEART. [*To Fu*]

• • •

BEST HAPPINESS OF ALL

I AM OLD AND I AM BORED. I WAS NEVER VERY WISE AND MY MIND HAS NEVER WALKED MUCH FURTHER THAN MY FEET. ONLY MY FOREST, MY FOREST . . . I GO BACK AND BACK TO WANDER THERE.

THERE BLUE FINGERS OF THE MOON STILL PLAY ON MY OLD LUTE. THERE WIND SCATTERS CLOUDS AND COMES DOWN TO FLUTTER MY ROBE.

YOU ASK ME WHAT IS THE BEST HAPPINESS OF ALL? IN THE FOREST IT IS SWEET TO HEAR A GIRL SINGING ON THE PATH, AFTER SHE HAS STOPPED TO ASK HER WAY, AND THANKED YOU WITH A SMILE.

[*Wang-Wei*]

• • •

THE BLUE ROBE

BRING ME NO MORE FLOWERS. BRING ME ONLY CYPRESS BOUGHS TO SHROUD MY FACE.

AFTER SUNSET IN THE MOUNTAINS, I WILL PUT ON MY BLUE ROBE WITH LONG SLEEVES, AND GO OUT TO SLEEP AMONG THE BAMBOOS THAT SHE LOVED.

[*Tu Fu*]

A FLUTE AT NIGHT

HERE ON THE FAR SOUTHERN BORDER THE SAND BELOW THE MOUNTAIN LIES LIKE A FIELD OF SNOW, THE MOONLIGHT IS LIKE FROST ALONG THE CITY-WALL. SOMEONE SOMEWHERE PLAYING ON HIS FLUTE HAS MADE THE NORTHERN SOLDIERS HOMESICK ALL NIGHT LONG. [*Li Yi*]

• • •

WATCHING AND WONDERING

HIGH ON A HILL, LOOKING DOWN ON THE WINDY LAKE. SEE: A LITTLE ROCKING BOAT, STORM-TOSSED LIKE OUR LIFE TOGETHER. NOW MIST HAS HIDDEN BOAT AND JOURNEY.

OVER THE MIST THE SUN SETS FAR OFF IN HEAVEN. ONLY HILLS ARE RED: FIELD, HOLLOW AND LAKE ARE BLUE WITH SHADOW.

NOW ISLANDS IN THE LAKE ARE BLACK PEARLS SET IN AMETHYST. NOW THAT WOODED HILL, A HEAD OF WAVING WOMAN'S HAIR, IS BLACK. AND SEE, A CRESCENT COMB OF SILVER MOON.

SAD AND HAPPY, I PICK UP MY LUTE AND SING UNTIL THE STARS GROW PALE. [*Tsiang-Tien*]

THE MAIDEN LO-FO

GOING TO GATHER LEAVES, LO-FO PUTS UP HER GLEAMING HAIR. SHE PUTS A PEARL IN EACH PEARL EAR; SHE WEARS A DRESS OF PINK AND A DRESS OF YELLOW. HER BASKET BEARS A LITTLE TWIST OF SILK.

ON THE SOUTH ROAD THE GOVERNOR OF THE PROVINCE CALLS TO HIS MEN TO STOP THE HORSES. "ASK THAT PRETTY ONE HER NAME. FIND OUT HER AGE FOR ME."

SAID LO-FO: "IN THE COUNTRYSIDE OF TSIN THERE LIVES A GIRL NAMED LO-FO. SHE IS NOT TWENTY YET, BUT NEITHER IS SHE A CHILD, FOR SHE HAS PASSED SIXTEEN."

THE GOVERNOR HESITATES. "ASK THE LOVELY MAIDEN IF SHE WISHES TO COME WITH ME IN MY CHARIOT."

LO-FO LOWERS HER BLACK EYES. "SURELY THE GOVERNOR HAS A WIFE IN THE SOUTH HE LOVES? SO EVEN IN TSIN, THE MAID LO-FO HAS HER YOUNG MAN WHOM SHE HAS PROMISED, WHOM SHE LOVES."

[*Anonymous*]

• • •

LOOKING INTO MIST

THE ASHES LIE CHILL AND GRAY IN THE GOLDEN BRAZIER. MY COVERLETS ROLL IN RED WAVES AS I TOSS IN MY BED. I THROW THEM OFF AWAY FROM ME; THEY FLOAT DOWN LIKE WAVES ON THE FLOOR. BUT I HAVE NO STRENGTH TO RISE AND BRUSH OUT MY LONG HAIR; EVEN THE JADE COMB IS TOO HEAVY FOR MY HAND. LET THE DUST SETTLE ON MY DRESSING-TABLE, DULLING MY GLEAMING BOTTLES.

NOW THE SUN BEGINS TO GLITTER THROUGH MY CURTAINS. ITS RISING WILL CAST BITTER SHADOWS OF SORROW IN MY HEART. I WISH TO SPEAK, I WANT TO CRY OUT; BUT FROM MY THROAT I CRUSH BACK MY CRIES INTO MY HEART. THIS IS NEW FOR ME, PAIN WHICH COMES NOT FROM TOO MUCH WINE, NOR FROM THE SADNESS OF APPROACHING AUTUMN.

NO, IT IS OVER NOW AND FINISHED. TODAY HE GOES AWAY. EVEN IF I SANG THE SWEET STAY-BY-ME SONG TO HIM TEN THOUSAND TIMES, HE WOULD NOT STAY. MY THOUGHTS MUST TRAVEL THE LONG ROAD TO THE SOUTH COUNTRY: HIS COUNTRY, VERY FAR AWAY.

SEE THE MIST AROUND MY PAVILION: BEFORE MY

EYES THERE IS MIST ALL ABOUT. IT IS THE IMAGE OF MY SADNESS, THE REFLECTION OF MY DULL, STILL EYES. FOREVER WILL MY DULL EYES STARE AT YOU, PALE MIST, MY EYES THAT NEVER WILL LIGHT UP AGAIN. [*Li Yi-hang*]

• • •

THE WILLOW LEAF

THAT MAIDEN, DREAMING AT HER WINDOW-LEDGE, LEANING ON HER SOFT WHITE ARMS . . . I DO NOT LOVE HER FOR HER GREAT MANSION ON THE SHORE OF THE YELLOW RIVER. I LOVE HER BECAUSE SHE HAS LET FALL, FLOATING DOWN INTO THE STREAM, A LITTLE WILLOW LEAF.

I DO NOT LOVE THE EAST WIND BECAUSE IT CARRIES TO ME THE SCENT OF THOSE PEACH-TREES THAT ARE LIKE SNOW ON THE MOUNTAINS. I LOVE IT BECAUSE IT HAS CARRIED THE LITTLE WILLOW LEAF TO MY BOAT.

AND THE LITTLE WILLOW LEAF . . . I DO NOT LOVE IT BECAUSE IT REMINDS ME THAT SOFT SPRING HAS COME AGAIN. I LOVE IT BECAUSE THE DREAMING MAIDEN HAS PICKED A NAME ON IT WTH HER NEEDLE, AND BECAUSE THAT NAME IS MINE. [*Chan Tiu-lin*]

AN UNHAPPY TIME

THE HOURS PASS . . . THE PHOENIX FLIES AND FLIES FROM HOME. STARLINGS AND SPARROWS BUILD THEIR NESTS IN THE ALTAR OF OUR ANCESTRAL HALL. MAGNOLIAS REACH OUT THEIR TENDRILS . . . THE JUNGLE SEIZES THEM, THEY PERISH ENTANGLED. RANCID SMELLS DRIVE OUT SWEET FRAGRANCES. EVERYWHERE THE EVIL PRINCIPLE HAS DISPOSSESSED THE GOOD.

THIS IS THE TIME OF BADNESS . . . LOYAL, BUT IN DESPAIR, I BEGIN MY JOURNEYS OF EXILE.

[*Chu Yuan*]

• • •

THE SHADOW OF A LEAF

ALONE IN HER ROOM A GIRL EMBROIDERS SILKEN FLOWERS. SHE HEARS A FLUTE AFAR. SHE SHIVERS . . . DREAMING A YOUNG MAN IS SINGING TO HER OF HIS LOVE.

FROM THE SUNLIGHT SLANTING THROUGH THE PAPER WINDOW, THE SHADOW OF AN ORANGE-LEAF FALLS ON HER BREAST. SHE CLOSES HER EYES. . . . DREAMING A YOUNG MAN'S HAND IS OPENING HER ROBE.

[*Ting Tun-ling*]

A LOYAL WIFE

YOUR LORDSHIP, I AM GRATFUL FOR THE TWO PEARLS YOU OFFER ME, BUT I TREMBLE WITH UNCERTAINTY. WHAT SHALL I SAY? . . . I SAY TO YOU: I AM MARRIED AND HAVE SWORN TO BE FAITHFUL TO MY HUSBAND.

PERHAPS YOU DO NOT KNOW THAT THE COLORS OF MY FAMILY HANG IN THE ROYAL PARK? PERHAPS YOU DO NOT KNOW THAT MY HUSBAND IS HONORARY LANCER IN THE PALACE?

I THINK YOU ARE SINCERE; I THINK YOU ARE HONORABLE. THEREFORE I HAVE PUT YOUR PEARLS AGAINST MY ROBE, AND I HAVE LOOKED AT THEM, AND SMILED. BUT TAKE THEM NOW AGAIN. PERHAPS YOU WILL TAKE THESE TWO TEARS AS WELL?

AH, WHY DID I NOT KNOW YOU THREE YEARS AGO THIS SPRING?

[*Tchang Tsi*]

• • •

THE EMPEROR WALKS

RECLINING IN THE GOLDEN CHAIR THE SON OF THE SKY IS BRIGHT AMONG HIS COUNSELORS. HIS JEWELS SHINE . . . HE IS FULL SUN WITHIN

SURROUNDING STARS. THE COUNSELORS SPEAK GRAVELY OF GRAVE THINGS, BUT THE EMPEROR'S MIND IS AWAY, AWAY.

IN A PAVILION ALL PORCELAIN SHE SITS AMONG HER MAIDENS . . . BRIGHT LILY AMONG PLAIN LEAVES. HER FAN FLOATS BACK AND FORTH WEARILY LIKE A WAVING LEAF. HER LORD STAYS TOO LONG AWAY.

PERFUME IS ON THE BREEZE . . . AN OPEN WINDOW IN THE COUNCIL-ROOM. THE EMPEROR DREAMS: SHE IS FANNING ME THE FLAVOR OF HER LIPS. HE RISES, GLITTERING WITH JEWELS, AND SLOWLY WALKS, WALKS TO THE PORCELAIN PAVILION. THE GRAVE COUNSELORS ARE LEFT, LOOKING AT EACH OTHER IN SUDDEN SILENCE.

[*Tu Fu*]

• • •

THE ENCOUNTER

THEY MET. THEIR EYES MET IN SHINING DUST AT THE CAPITAL. HE RAISED HIS RIDING-CROP IN GOLDEN GREETING. "OF ALL THOSE TEN THOUSAND HOUSES BY THE WILLOWED RIVER, FAIR SWEET LADY, WHICH IS THE LITTLE ONE YOU CALL HOME?"

[*Li Po*]

THE BREATH OF SPRING

THE BREATH OF SPRING IS EVERYWHERE, IN EVERY FACE. THE MIMOSA CASTS ITS DELICATE SHADOWS . . . MY DREAMS ARE BUTTERFLIES . . . THE FRAGRANCE OF THE QUINCE INTOXICATES LIKE WINE.

BUT I PLUCK THE WILLOW OF SORROW. A GULF DIVIDES US, AND THERE IS NO FAIRY BRIDGE OF BIRDS TO CARRY ME ACROSS.

I WEEP ALONE BEFORE MY SILVER LAMP AND GROW FRAIL AS HSIAO YAN THE SLENDER BEAUTY. WHEN SHALL WE SHARE A NIGHT LIKE THIS, A SPRING NIGHT LIKE THIS, AND MEET TOGETHER UNDER A FULL MOON? [*Anonymous*]

• • •

JADE FLOWER PALACE

HERE BY THE WINDING STREAMLET, AMONG THE SIGHING WINDS, OLD GRAY MICE SCURRY OVER THE ROOF-TILES. NO ONE ANY MORE REMEMBERS THE PRINCE'S NAME WHO BUILT THIS PALACE UNDER OVERHANGING CLIFFS.

IN DARKENED ROOMS YOU CAN SEE GREEN GHOST FIRES . . . FROM THE FLUTES OF THE FOREST YOU

CAN HEAR A THOUSAND VOICES. THE YOUNG PALACE LADIES OF LONG AGO ARE IN THEIR YELLOW GRAVES . . . THEN WHY ARE PAINTED SCROLLS STILL HANGING ON THE WALL? THE CHARIOTEERS AND THEIR GOLD CHARIOTS ARE CRUMBLED . . . THEN WHY ARE STONE HORSES, CARVED IN OLDEN DAYS, STANDING YET?

SADNESS SITS ON THE GRASS. I SING THE STORY, BUT I AM HEAVY WITH SORROW . . . AMONG ALL THESE PATHS THAT WE MAY WALK ALONG INTO THE DISTANCE, WHICH ONE WILL EVER CARRY US TO LIFE FOREVER? [*Tu Fu*]

• • •

WINE-FLASK AT SUNSET

SPRING FRAGRANCES, AND LEVEL SUN-SHAFTS, COME SIFTING THROUGH MY SHUTTERS. NOW COMES THE SUPPER-HOUR WHEN BOATMEN BOIL THEIR RICE ON THE RIVER. IN THE GARDEN SPARROWS ARE TWITTERING . . . ON THE ROAD A CHARIOT-WHEEL IS GRATING.

NOW FOR THE WINE-FLASK. LET MY TROUBLES FLY AWAY . . . JOINING THE INSECTS A-BUZZ IN THE LATE-SUN GARDEN. [*Tu Fu*]

WHEN THE SUN ROSE....

WHEN SHE WENT OUT TO MEET HER LOVER UNDER THE BIG WILLOW TREE BY THE RIVER EDGE, SHE PUT ON TWO OF HER LOVELY ROBES TO PLEASE HIM.

WHEN THE SUN SANK BELOW THE HILLS, AND THE NIGHT WAS DARK, THE TWO LOVERS STILL LAY THERE, TALKING TENDERLY TOGETHER.

SUDDENLY SHE ROSE TO HER FEET, ROSY WITH SHAME. HER THIRD ROBE, THE DARKNESS UNDER THE WILLOW, HAD FALLEN OFF WITH DAWN. . . .

[*Li Chuang-chia*]

• • •

GOING TO MARKET

THE LITTLE SERVANT-BOY . . . TYING THE FEET OF THE CHICKEN HE WILL TAKE TO MARKET. THE CHICKEN FLUTTERS IN HIS HANDS, AND SQUAWKS WITH FRIGHT.

MY FATHER STARES WITHOUT FEELINGS. MY MOTHER TURNS AWAY HER HEAD. A SPARROW OVERHEAD IS ACTING SO DELIGHTED . . . MAYBE SOME EXTRA GRAIN FOR HIM?

[*Tu Fu*]

LIKE A CORMORANT

THE CORMORANT STANDS STILL, THINKING, ALL ALONE AT THE RIVER'S EDGE. HIS STARING EYE FOLLOWS THE CHANGING WATERS.

WHEN STROLLERS COME TOO CLOSE TO HIM, BALANCING HIS LONG NECK HE FLAPS AWAY, WAITING IN THE TALL REEDS TILL THE INTRUDERS PASS . . . WISHING TO STARE AGAIN AT THE UNDULATIONS OF THE STREAM.

AND AT DUSK, WHEN THE MOON IS RIPPLING ON THE WAVES, THE CORMORANT STILL STANDS, THINKING, WITH ONE FOOT IN THE CURRENT . . . JUST SO A MAN, HIS HEART BURNING WITH PASSION, STARES AT THE UNDULATIONS OF HIS DREAM.

[*Su Tong po*]

• • •

TROUBLED WATERS

THE AUTUMN MOON IS DANCING IN THE GREEN WATERS OF LAKE NAN-HOU. NOW THE SOUND OF MY OARS HAS TROUBLED THE LOVE-SONG OF WHITE WATER-LILIES SINGING TO THE MOON.

[*Li Po*]

CAPTIVITY

IN THE OLD DAYS, IN THE PALACE HUNG WITH PAINTED SCROLLS, IT WAS A GOOD LIFE FOR ME. INCENSE BURNED WHERE I WALKED, SILK CUSHIONS WERE SCATTERED WHERE I SLEPT, MUSICIANS PLAYED ABOUT ME . . . I LOOKED OUT ON GARDENS WITH PATHS OF CORAL PEBBLES.

NOW, PRISONER IN THIS COLD FORTRESS, I HEAR ONLY FRIGHTENING CALLS FROM THE WATCHMAN, SILLY CRIES FROM MONKEYS PLAYING ON BARE ROCKS IN MOONLIGHT.

FEAR SHAKES ME. MY GUTS ARE EMPTIED OF COURAGE. IF ONLY I COULD SEE THE LIGHTS OF THE CAPITAL! . . . BUT ALL I CAN SEE ARE STARS ABOVE IT.

I SIT ON THE STONE FORTRESS WALL . . . THERE, WINDS BRING SCENT OF ALMOND BLOSSOMS FROM TREES BEYOND MY SIGHT.

[*Tu Fu*]

• • •

BE CAREFUL

TAKE CARE, BE FEARFUL, NIGHT AND DAY LOOK SHARP . . . WE DO NOT STUMBLE ON MOUNTAINS, BUT ON CLODS, AND FALL.

[*Anonymous*]

AUTUMN OF ALL GOOD THINGS

OUT ON THE MOUNTAIN-SIDES, WHIRLING DEAD LEAVES ARE ABROAD. COME WITH ME, UP HERE ON THIS WATCH-TOWER. . . . HERE, AT THE SEA'S EDGE, WE CAN WATCH GRAY CLOUDS TORN BY WINDS, AND BE SAD TOGETHER NOW AUTUMN HAS RETURNED.

ONCE MORE THE TARTAR HORDES ARE GATHERING ON THE KOBI BORDER. ONCE MORE WE SEE THE AMBASSADOR FROM HAN COME HOME, RIDING THROUGH THE IMPERIAL GATE. BUT WILL WE EVER SEE COME HOME ALL THE MEN THAT WAR HAS SUMMONED? [*Li Po*]

• • •

THE FORMER WIFE SPEAKS

BED-CURTAIN, LONG FLAPPING IN THE BREEZE AT NIGHT, LONG HANGING THERE TO SCREEN US IN THE DAY! WHEN I LEFT MY FATHER'S HOUSE I BROUGHT YOU WITH ME AND UNFOLDED YOU WITH DELIGHT. NOW I AM TAKING YOU BACK AGAIN. I FOLD YOU AND LAY YOU FLAT IN THIS WOODEN BOX. BED-CURTAIN, WILL I EVER UNFOLD YOU AND HANG YOU UP AGAIN?

[*Wife of Lieu Hsun*]

FADING IN THE SPRINGTIME

THE CAREFUL KNOT OF HAIR LIES LOW UPON HER NECK; HER LONG AND NARROW EYEBROWS ARE PAINTED SKILLFULLY.

ALAS! FOLLOWING YOU, HER THOUGHTS ARE WANDERING AFAR; IN THIS SEASON OF A HUNDRED FLOWERS, SHE GROWS THIN AND PALE.

[*Weng T'ing-chun*]

• • •

THE GIRL AT HOME

EARTH HAS SWALLOWED THE SNOW. AGAIN WE SEE PLUM-TREES IN BLOSSOM. NEW WILLOW-LEAVES ARE GOLD. COLD WATERS OF THE LAKE ARE SILVER . . . BUTTERFLIES POWDERED WITH GOLD LAY VELVET HEADS TO THE HEARTS OF FLOWERS.

IN HIS UNMOVING BOAT THE YOUNG FISHERMAN PULLS UP HIS DRIPPING NET, MAKING RIPPLES ON THE STILL WATER.

HE THINKS OF A GIRL AT HOME, LIKE A DARK SWALLOW IN ITS NEST. HE THINKS OF A GIRL AT HOME, WAITING LIKE A DARK SWALLOW FOR HER MATE.

[*Li Po*]

THE DRAGONFLY

DRAGONFLY WINGS . . . SHINING SILKEN GARMENTS. NOW MY HEART IS ACHING. WHO WILL GIVE IT REST?

YOUNG DRAGONFLY WINGS . . . RICH EMBROIDERED GARMENTS. NOW MY HEART IS ACHING. WHO WILL GIVE IT PEACE?

DRAGONFLY BURSTING ITS COCOON . . . PLAIN WHITE LINEN GARMENTS. NOW MY HEART IS ACHING. WHO WILL GIVE IT LOVE?

[*The Book of Songs*]

• • •

WE WILL GROW OLD TOGETHER

OVER AND OVER YOU SAID: "WE WILL GROW OLD TOGETHER. TOGETHER, THE SAME TIME, YOUR HAIR AND MY HAIR WILL TURN WHITE LIKE SNOW, WHITE LIKE A MIDSUMMER MOON." TODAY, MY LORD, I HAVE HEARD THAT YOU LOVE ANOTHER WOMAN . . . WITH MY HEART BROKEN I COME TO SAY GOODBYE.

ONE LAST TIME LET US POUR THE OLD WINE INTO OUR TWO CUPS. ONE LAST TIME LET YOU SING ME THE SAD SONG OF THE DEAD BIRD UNDER THE

SNOW . . . THEN I WILL TAKE BOAT AND SAIL DOWN THE RIVER YU CHEU, WHOSE WATERS DIVIDE TO FLOW HALF EAST, HALF WEST.

WHY DO YOU CRY, YOUNG GIRLS ABOUT TO MARRY? WHY DO YOU CRY? PERHAPS YOU WILL MARRY A LOYAL MAN WITH A FAITHFUL HEART, WHO WILL SAY TO YOU SOLEMNLY OVER AND OVER: "WE WILL GROW OLD TOGETHER." [*Li Po*]

• • •

AT HSIEN-YU TEMPLE

THE TALL CRANE WALKED OUT OF THE POOL AND STOOD ON THE FLIGHT OF STEPS. THE MOON DANCED OUT OF THE POOL AND ENTERED THE OPEN DOOR.

I WAS ENTRANCED BY THIS PLACE . . . I COULD NOT LEAVE FOR TWO NIGHTS.

FORTUNATE TO FIND A PLACE SO PEACEFUL . . . HAPPY NO COMPANION WAS THERE TO DRAG ME HOME!

NOW I HAVE FOUND THIS PEACEFUL LONELINESS, I HAVE RESOLVED TO COME HERE ONLY WITH MYSELF. [*Po Chu-i*]

THE AUTUMN WIND

THE WIND BLOWS, THE WHITE CLOUDS RUN, THE GRASS PALES, THE TREES FALL BARE, THE GEESE FLY SOUTH. BUT THE ORCHIDS BLOOM, CHRYSANTHEMUMS GIVE THEIR SCENT. I THINK OF MY LOVELY GIRL. I MUST LEAVE HER, BUT I CAN NOT FORGET.

I AM ROWED ACROSS THE RIVER ON MY PLEASURE BARGE, ACROSS THE RIVER WITH WHITE WAVES RISING. FLUTE AND DRUM AND ROWERS' SONG GO WITH ME. NOW THE FEASTING, NOW THE DANCING . . . BUT STILL MY HEART IS SAD AND WILL NOT DANCE.

HOW FEW OUR YEARS OF GOLDEN YOUTH! HOW CERTAIN OUR GRAY YEARS OF AGE!

[*Emperor Wu-ti*]

• • •

THE END OF ALL

CLEAN THE OCTOBER WIND. CLEAR THE OCTOBER MOON. HEAPED BROWN LEAVES ARE BLOWING . . . A BLACK RAVEN FLIES FROM ITS ICY ROOST.

I DREAM OF YOU. WILL EVER I SEE YOU AGAIN? AH, NIGHT OF SORROWING HEART! [*Li Po*]

WAITING ON THE TOWER

HERE THE MOON FLOATS BRIGHT OVER HEAVEN'S MOUNTAIN; IT SAILS ON A WHITE-CLOUD OCEAN. FIVE THOUSAND MILES AWAY A SHRILL WIND'S SCREAMING . . . AND COLD IS WHISTLING FROM YU-MEN PASS.

THE EMPEROR'S SOLDIERS MARCH DOWN WHITE MOUND ROAD. TARTARS SEARCH THE INLETS OF THE BLUE SEA. SOLDIERS MAY TURN THEIR HEADS, THINKING OF HOME, BUT AT HOME WE NEVER SEE A RETURNING SOLDIER.

SHE IS STANDING ON THE WATCH-TOWER AGAIN TONIGHT. SORROW AND SADNESS WITHOUT END . . . IS ALL.

[*Li Po*]

• • •

THE WOMEN OF PA

UP HERE AT PA, THE RIVER SHOOTS LIKE FLYING ARROWS. LET A BOAT BE CAUGHT AND IT'S SWEPT OFF A THOUSAND MILES BEFORE THE CURRENT QUIETS DOWN.

O YOU WOMEN OF PA! HOW LUCKY FOR US YOUR HUSBANDS MUST POLE UP THIS MIGHTY RIVER TO GET HOME!

[*Li Po*]

THE UNREWARDED POET

HERE SIT I ON A HARD WOOD BOX, STENCILED BLACK WITH THE NAME OF A SELLER OF SUGAR. THIS TABLE IS SO DIRTY . . . EVEN IF I HAD FOOD, I COULD NOT EAT IT HERE.

THEN HOW CAN I WRITE OF WINE SPRINKLED WITH VIOLETS, SO YOU MAY DRINK WITH DELIGHT? HOW CAN I PROMISE: I WILL DECORATE YOUR BLUE DRESS WITH GLITTERING EMERALD JEWELS? HOW CAN I OFFER YOU A PERFECT PEAR OF GOLDEN AMBER? OR POUR PERFUMES IN A CARVED BOWL OF ROSY QUARTZ, SO YOU MAY DIP IN IT THE POINTED TIPS OF THOSE BELOVÈD PALE FINGERS?

[*J. Wing*]

• • •

TO HIS DEAD LOVER

THE SWISHING SOUND OF SILK IS STILL. THE DUST GATHERS ON MARBLE FLOORS. THE ROOM IS HOLLOW, COLD AND SILENT. LEAVES HAVE DRIFTED AGAINST THE DOORS.

LONGING FOR THAT LOST SWEET GIRL, I WONDER HOW TO LULL MY ACHING HEART TO REST.

[*Li Fu-jen*]

TO THE HERMIT CHENG

I HEAR YOU HAVE COME HERE TO LIVE FOR GOOD . . . HERE BY THE LONELY GATE, AMONG THE BURIAL MOUNDS, ENCLOSED BY TALL BAMBOO GROVES.

I HAVE COME NOW TO ASK A FAVOR: WILL YOU LEND ME YOUR OLD GARDEN, TO USE FOR LOOKING AT THE HILLS?

[*Po Chu-i*]

• • •

NON-BEING

JOIN THE SPOKES TOGETHER TO MAKE A WHEEL. A WHEEL IS FULL OF OPENNESS . . . NON-BEING. BUT IT IS NECESSARY.

SPIN WET CLAY TO SHAPE A COOKING-POT. A COOKING-POT IS EMPTY . . . FULL OF NON-BEING. BUT IT IS NECESSARY.

WORK A SAW TO CUT OUT DOOR AND WINDOWS. DOOR AND WINDOWS ARE HOLES . . . NON-BEING. BUT THEY ARE NECESSARY.

TO HAVE BEING IS GOOD. BUT ALSO IT IS NECESSARY TO HAVE NON-BEING . . . NOTHINGNESS.

[*The Way of Virtue*]

ETERNITY

THE HEAVEN ENDURES FOREVER AND THE EARTH IS ETERNAL. WHY ARE HEAVEN AND EARTH ENDURING AND ETERNAL? BECAUSE THEY DO NOT LIVE FOR THEMSELVES . . . THEREFORE THEY CAN LIVE FOREVER.

THE WISE MAN DESIRES TO BE FORGOTTEN, BUT HE IS REMEMBERED. HE DESIRES TO BE FREE OF LIFE, BUT HE RETAINS IT. HE DESIRES NOTHING FOR HIMSELF, BUT HE FINDS EVERYTHING HE WANTS. [*The Way of Virtue*]

• • •

THE WAY OF THE WAY

IF YOU FOLLOW THE WAY, YOU MAY TRAVEL ALL OVER THE EMPIRE WITHOUT HARM. YOU WILL FIND PEACE AND YOU WILL FIND QUIETNESS.

PERHAPS YOU WILL PAUSE FOR MUSIC AND STRANGE FOODS . . . NO HARM TO ENJOY THEM.

BUT THE WAY ITSELF HAS NO FLAVOR, THE WAY ITSELF HAS NO SOUND, THE WAY ITSELF CANNOT BE SEEN . . . BUT USE IT: IT IS NEVER ENDING.

[*The Way of Virtue*]

AWAY WITH PHILOSOPHERS

AWAY WITH PHILOSOPHERS, AWAY WITH SAGES. PEOPLE WILL BE A HUNDREDFOLD WISER . . . AWAY WITH CHARITY, AWAY WITH VIRTUE. PEOPLE WILL RETURN TO GOODNESS AND KINDNESS. . . . AWAY WITH PROFITS, AWAY WITH SKILLS. PEOPLE WILL BE FREE OF ROBBERS AND THIEVES.

IF THESE THREE REFORMS ARE NOT ENOUGH, THEN LET ALL MEN SIMPLY GAZE ON PLAINNESS, CHERISH UNCARVED BLOCKS OF STONE, FORGO THE "I," AND FREE THEMSELVES FROM ALL DESIRE. [*The Way of Virtue*]

• • •

NOT IN REPAYMENT

HE GAVE ME A QUINCE. THEN I GAVE HIM A CARVED JADE . . . NOT TO PAY HIM BACK, BUT TO MAKE OUR LOVE LONG-LASTING.

HE GAVE ME A PEACH. THEN I GAVE HIM AN EMERALD . . . NOT TO PAY HIM BACK, BUT TO MAKE OUR LOVE LONG-LASTING.

HE GAVE ME A PLUM. THEN I GAVE HIM A BLACK JADE . . . NOT TO PAY HIM BACK, BUT TO MAKE OUR LOVE LONG-LASTING. [*The Book of Songs*]

WAITING FOR YOU

OVER THE PASS OF THE WESTERN MOUNTAINS TRAVELS THE EVENING SUN; THE HILL-FOLDS GATHER THEIR DEEP DARK; THE MOON LIGHTS UP COLD IN ITS TWISTED PINE-BRANCH; THE LITTLE BROOK SINGS COLD, AND THE COLD WIND SIGHS; THE WOOD-CUTTERS ALL HAVE CARRIED THEIR BUNDLES HOME; THE WHEELING BIRDS ARE SETTLED IN THEIR TREES.

THE HOUR IS PAST THAT YOU PROMISED YOU WOULD COME. MY LUTE IS STILL . . . LEANING AMONG THE VINES, WAITING IN THE COLD GLEN AMONG THE VINES. [*Mêng Hai-jan*]

• • •

DRAGON OF THE SHORELESS SEA

OH DRAGON, RULER OF THE SHORELESS SEA OF DEATH, CARRY AWAY MY BELOVÈD, WHILE, LEANING OVER HER WITH PASSION, I DRINK IN HER PERFUMED BREATH.

CARRY HER AWAY IN YOUR SHIP OF GHOSTS, AND CARRY ME AWAY WITH HER . . . THAT WE MAY FLOAT FOREVER TOGETHER ON THAT SEA, DRUNKEN WITH LOVE [*Li Hung-chang*]

THE WIND-TORN ROOF

IN THE EIGHTH-MOON OF AUTUMN, WITH A VICIOUS HOWLING, WIND TORE THREE LAYERS OF THATCH FROM MY POOR ROOF.

FLYING OVER THE RIVER THE THATCH RAINED ON THE EMBANKMENT, TANGLED IN THE TREES, WHIRLED AFAR TO SINK AND SETTLE IN THE MARSHES.

A SWARM OF BOYS FROM THE VILLAGE LAUGHED AT ME BECAUSE I AM FEEBLE. O INSOLENCE! STEALING MY THATCH AND CARRYING IT OFF TO PLAY WITH IN THE BAMBOO GROVE! I SCREAMED AT THEM WITH A DRY TONGUE . . . BUT THEY LAUGHED AT ME AND I CAME HOME SIGHING.

THEN THE WIND STOPPED, THE CLOUDS TURNED DARK, AND NIGHT CAME ON LIKE INK. MY OLD COTTON QUILT WAS COLD AS IRON . . . MY SWEET SON TOSSED IN HIS SLEEP, BARE FEET STICKING THROUGH THE BLANKET . . . RAIN CAME THROUGH THE ROOF TILL THERE WAS NOT A DRY INCH IN BED.

LIKE STRINGS OF WAX THE RAIN HUNG DOWN . . . ALL THESE DISASTERS OF WAR HANG DOWN AND KEEP US FROM PEACEFUL REST.

I DREAM OF A GREAT HOUSE WITH TEN THOUSAND ROOMS. THERE ALL COLD CREATURES CAN TAKE SHELTER, WITH BRIGHT FACES, OUT OF THE RAIN, OUT OF THE WIND, SAFE IN A HOUSE SOLID AS A MOUNTAIN.

AH, WHEN SHALL I EVER SEE SUCH A HOUSE? COULD I EVER SEE IT. . . . AH, THOUGH THE WIND TORE DOWN MY HUT ENTIRELY, THOUGH I FROZE TO DEATH IN THE STORM, THEN SHOULD I DIE HAPPY.

[*Tu Fu*]

• • •

THE STARTLED PLUMS FALL DOWN

THE CLOUDS ARE SOFT, THE WILLOWS DELICATE . . . HER HAIR IS FRESHLY DRESSED. SHE PLACES THE FLUTE UPON HER LIPS, AND AS THE SUNSET FADES AND DUSK SETTLES, SHE PLAYS BENEATH THE PALE MOON.

A FRESHLY-OPENED CHERRY BUD . . . HER LIPS UPON THE FLUTE. SHE LEANS IN THE CORNER OF THE BALCONY: THE NIGHT IS CHILL, HER SILKEN ROBES ARE THIN, HER FINGERS COLD . . . BUT MUSIC FLOATS THROUGH FROSTY WOODS AND STARTLED PLUMS FALL PATTERING DOWN.

[*Chang Hsien*]

WEEP NOT, YOUNG WOMEN

IT IS ALWAYS SAD AUTUMN WHEN OUR ENEMIES SWEEP DOWN THEIR RAIDERS FROM THE MOUNTAINS TO INVADE US.

THE TRUMPETS SUMMON THE WARRIORS! THEY WILL RIDE ON TILL THEY COME TO THE GREAT WALL. THEN THEY WILL RIDE BEYOND IT, OUT ON THE GREAT KOBI DESERT.

THERE, ONLY THE COLD BARE MOON. ONLY COLD BEADS OF DEW ON SWORDS AND SHIELDS. HOW THEY SHIVER!

WEEP NOT, YOUNG WOMEN . . . THIS IS NO TIME TO START YOUR WEEPING. WHO KNOWS HOW LONG THAT YOU MUST WEEP? [*Li Po*]

• • •

BEFORE AND AFTER

LOOKING BACKWARD . . . I CANNOT SEE THE ANCIENTS OF DAYS. LOOKING FORWARD . . . I CANNOT SEE AGES YET TO COME. ONLY HEAVEN AND EARTH HAVE REMAINED, AND WILL REMAIN FOREVER . . . I AM ALONE, I GRIEVE, I DROP TEARS INTO THE DUST. [*Chen Tzu-ang*]

WHY BE JEALOUS?

MY LITTLE BOAT IS MADE OF EBONY; MY FLUTE-STOPS ARE PURE GOLD. WATER LOOSENS STAINS FROM SILK . . . WINE LOOSENS SADNESS FROM THE HEART.

WITH GOOD WINE, A GRACEFUL BOAT, AND A SWEET GIRL'S LOVE . . . WHY BE JEALOUS OF MERE GODS?

[*Li Po*]

• • •

A LADY FROM AFAR

THAT NIGHT . . . A NIGHT IN EARLY AUTUMN . . . WE SAILED TO THE ISLE OF PARROTS. THERE WE GAZED AT THE ROUND MOON, AND LISTENED TO THE WINDY PINES.

SUDDENLY WE HEARD MUSIC . . . A SAD SONG COMING ON THE WIND. THERE WAS A SINGER IN A BOAT.

AS IT DREW NEAR US WE SAW A WOMAN, WHITE AS SNOW, SINGING AND CRYING TOO, LEANING ON THE MAST. MY COMPANIONS ASKED HER WHY SHE WEPT? . . . WITHOUT AN ANSWER SHE LOWERED HER HEAD, VEILING HER WHITE FACE IN HER GOLDEN HAIR.

[*Pe Kin-yi*]

TO THE DANCING-GIRL SIAO-LING

YOU CALLED FOR POEMS ABOUT TWILIGHT. EACH TWILIGHT NOW BRINGS MEMORIES OF THE SOFT BLUE DRESS YOU WORE . . . THAT DAY IN THE PALACE WHEN YOU READ AND JUDGED THEM.

IF MINE WAS JUDGED THE BEST . . . YOU SEE, THERE WAS A VISION OF YOU, A VISION IN BLUE VEILS, IN THE BLUE DAWN WHEN I COULD NOT SLEEP. SO I GOT UP FROM BED AND WROTE THE POEM FOR YOU . . .

BUT YOU SLEPT ON UNKNOWING IN THAT EARLY DAWN. YOU DID NOT PEEP OUT FROM THE JADE FLOWER PAVILION TO SEE ROSES BLOOMING IN THE SKY ABOVE THE PALACE. IN THAT SAME PALACE ONCE, FOR LOVE OF HER, WOU-TI MADE EMPRESS A LOVELY DANCING-GIRL LIKE YOU.

[*Tsiang-Tien*]

• • •

THE GARDEN THAT DOES NOT FADE

THESE FLOWERS OF JADE IN THEIR LITTLE BOX . . . MAY YOUR NOBLE THOUGHTS, LIKE THESE FLOWERS, BE ALWAYS INDESTRUCTIBLE AND LOVINGLY ARRANGED. [*Emperor Chien Lung*]

PEASANT SONG

WHEN THE SUN RISES, WE GET UP TO WORK. WHEN THE SUN SETS, WE LIE DOWN TO SLEEP. FOR OUR WATER WE DIG OUR WELLS, FOR OUR FOOD WE HOE OUR FIELDS. O THE EMPEROR MAY BE GREAT AND POWERFUL, BUT WHAT IS THAT TO US?

[*Anonymous*]

• • •

THE POET DREAMS

NOW SAD RAINS ARE FALLING. LET US SAY NOW: THE SKY WEEPS BECAUSE FINE WEATHER IS ALL GONE. BOREDOM PILES UP LIKE HEAVY RAIN-CLOUDS: WHERE IS OUR GAIETY AND WIT? LET US SIT INDOORS.

NOW IS THE TIME FOR POETRY THAT REMEMBERS SUMMER. LET IT BE PUT DOWN GENTLY ON WHITE PAPER, LIKE FULL-BLOWN PETALS FALLING FROM EXQUISITE TREES. AND LET MY LIPS DRINK FROM THIS CUP OF SUMMER WINE EACH TIME MY BRUSH IS DIPPED INTO THE INK. THUS WILL I KEEP MY FANCY FROM FLOATING OFF LIKE CLOUDS OR SMOKE: TIME PAST ESCAPES FROM US QUICKER THAN A FLIGHT OF BIRDS.

[*Tu Fu*]

LAUGHTER IN THE THICKET

THE GAY AND GALLANT YOUTH . . . HIS PALACE IS ON THE ROAD OF IMPERIAL TOMBS NEAR THE GOLDEN BAZAAR . . . SETS OUT INTO THE SWEET SPRING BREEZE.

HIS TALL WHITE CHARGER, SADDLED WITH SILVER, PRANCES GRACEFULLY IN RHYTHMIC STEPS. BENEATH HIM IS A WHIRLWIND OF PETALS AS HE RIDES THROUGH THE CARPET OF FALLEN BLOSSOMS.

THE YOUTH REINS IN THE CHARGER, PERPLEXED. . . . A LAUGH, SWEET AND MUSICAL, RINGS FROM THE THICKET; NOW HE IS PERPLEXED NO MORE.

[*Li Po*]

• • •

SEEING YOU OFF

BECAUSE YOU ARE OLD, BECAUSE YOU ARE LEAVING, MY HANDKERCHIEF IS WET WITH TEARS . . . BECAUSE YOU ARE SEVENTY YEARS OLD AND HAVE NO HOME.

I AM UNEASY AS THE WIND RISES AND YOUR BOAT SAILS OFF . . . WHITE-HEADED TRAVELER AMONG WHITE-HEADED WAVES.

[*Po Chu-i*]

A LETTER HOME

YOU ASK ME: WHEN WILL I COME HOME? THERE IS NO DATE SETTLED YET. HERE, AT PA-SHAN IN AUTUMN, EVENING RAIN FLOODS THE HOLLOWS.

O FOR THE TIME WHEN WE CAN PUT OUT THE CANDLE TOGETHER BY THE WESTERN WINDOW... O FOR THE TIME WHEN I CAN TELL YOU HOW I FEEL HERE TONIGHT AT PA-SHAN, WHEN AUTUMN RAIN FLOODS THE HOLLOWS.

[*Li Shang-yin*]

• • •

THE POET AND THE FLOOD

ICY WINDS SWEEP DOWN FROM THE MOUNTAINS AND RIP OUT THE TREES. PITILESS, THE FLOOD RISES IN THE RIVER DAY BY DAY. THERE IS NO MOUNTAIN NOW, OR FIELDS . . . EVERYTHING IS FOG AND WATER.

ALL THE SAME, MY LATE CHRYSANTHEMUMS ARE IN BLOOM. WHEN YOU ROW PAST, YUNG-HI, SLOW YOUR BOAT IN FRONT OF MY GARDEN AND GAZE AT THEM . . . THEIR HOT COLORS WILL REWARM YOUR HEART.

[*Tu Fu*]

PARTING IN AUTUMN

THE CRICKETS ARE COLD, THEIR SONG IS SAD. OUTSIDE THE PAVILION THE LAST SHOWER-DROPS PATTER DOWN. HOLLOW THE HAPPY FAREWELL PARTY. WE LINGER . . . WHILE THE RIVER-BOAT, LOADED WITH SANDALWOOD, IS WAITING FOR ME TO GO ABOARD.

WE STAND HAND IN HAND, WE STAND WITHOUT TALKING, WE STAND WITH TEARS . . . TO THINK THAT I MUST TRAVEL A THOUSAND MILES OF MIST AND RAIN AND WATER! THE EVENING CLOUDS ARE GATHERING AGAIN, AND THE SKY WIDENS TO THE SOUTH.

IT IS AN OLD STORY: PARTING FROM A LOVER IS FULL OF PAIN . . . AND IT IS ALL THE WORSE IN RAINY AUTUMN. TONIGHT, WHEN I GROW SOBER AFTER ALL THIS WINE, WHERE WILL YOU BE? ON THE WILLOWY SHORE, UNDER THE WANING MOON?

AND I . . . ALL THIS YEAR AWAY, SUNSHINE AND LOVELY SIGHTS WILL COME TO ME IN VAIN . . . NO ONE ALL THIS YEAR TO TELL A THOUSAND HAPPY THOUGHTS.

[*Li Yung*]

• • •

THE EMBROIDERY

THE COOL WIND OF EVENING BLOWS BIRD-SONG TO A WINDOW WHERE THE MAIDEN SITS. SHE IS EMBROIDERING FLOWER-PATTERNS ON SILK.

HER HEAD IS RAISED; HER WORK FALLS FROM HER FINGERS; HER THOUGHTS HAVE FLOWN TO SOMEONE FAR AWAY.

"A BIRD CAN EASILY FIND ITS MATE AMONG THE LEAVES, BUT ALL A MAIDEN'S TEARS, FALLING LIKE RAIN FROM HEAVEN, WILL NOT BRING BACK HER DISTANT LOVER."

SHE BENDS AGAIN TO HER EMBROIDERY: "I WILL WEAVE A LITTLE VERSE AMONG THESE FLOWERS OF HIS ROBE . . . PERHAPS HE WILL READ IT AND COME BACK AGAIN."

[*Li Po*]

• • •

THE SOUTH WIND

THE SWEET SMELL OF THE SOUTH WIND CAN CALM THE TEMPERS OF MY PEOPLE.

THE SWEET RAIN OF THE SOUTH WIND CAN NOURISH THE GRAIN-FIELDS OF MY PEOPLE.

[*Anonymous*]

LET US DRINK WINE

LOOK: DO YOU NOT SEE THE RAIN FALLING AT LAST FROM THE SKY? FALLING INTO THE YELLOW RIVER, FLOWING FAST INTO THE SEA, AND NEVER NEVER RETURNING?

LOOK: DO YOU NOT SEE THE CLEAR MIRROR IN THE HALL, SHOWING OUR HAIR BLACK SILK AT MORNING, FALLEN TO BITTER SNOW BY NIGHT?

YOU WHO HAVE HAD YOUR FILL OF BITTER LIFE, COME DRINK THE DREGS WITH ME! LET THERE BE MOONLIGHT IN OUR EVENING . . . LET THE GOLDEN CUPS NEVER STAND EMPTY.

HEAVEN BLESSED ME WITH RICHES AND I MUST SPEND MYSELF. THOUGH I THROW AWAY TEN THOUSAND GOLD COINS AND POEMS, ALWAYS I FIND MORE. SO LET US SLAUGHTER THE SHEEP AND THE OX . . . LET US MAKE MERRY AND MERRY . . . WHY, I PROMISE TO SWALLOW THREE HUNDRED CUPS THIS SINGLE NIGHT.

COME, FRIEND CH'IN . . . COME, MASTER CH'AN . . . I OFFER YOU MY WINE: DO NOT REFUSE IT. I OFFER YOU MY SONG: DO NOT IGNORE IT.

THE MEATS AND THE DANCING AND THE MUSIC ARE NOT MY DESIRE . . . MY ONLY DESIRE IS TO

BE DRUNK FOR EVER AND EVER AND NEVER WAKE AGAIN. SCHOLARS AND SAINTS ARE FORGOTTEN SOON; BUT GREAT DRUNKARDS ARE IMMORTAL.

THEY SAY PRINCE CH'EN AT HIS GREAT PING-YUEH TEMPLE FEAST PAID TEN THOUSAND COINS FOR WINE, SO EVERYONE COULD HAVE ENOUGH. NOW THAT I GIVE THE FEAST . . . DARE I LACK MONEY? NO! LET US BUY THE WINE! LET US DRINK TOGETHER! I WILL SEND MY BOY WITH MY FIVE-COLORED HORSE, I WILL SEND MY BOY WITH MY WONDROUS FURS WORTH ALONE TEN THOUSAND COINS . . . HE WILL BARTER THEM FOR WINE . . . AND WE, WE WILL DROWN THE SORROW OF A THOUSAND GENERATIONS! [*Li Po*]

• • •

AT THE RIVER

SHE GATHERS LILY-FLOWERS IN THE SHALLOW RIVER-WATERS . . . SINGING AS SHE WADES. NOW A STRANGER DAWDLES ALONG THE BANK. SHE TURNS AROUND TO LOOK AT HIM.

HIDING IN A BUNCH OF LILIES, PRETENDING TO BE EMBARRASSED . . . SHE PEEKS OUT TO SMILE.

[*Li Po*]

CHRYSANTHEMUMS

I BUILT MY LITTLE HOUSE RIGHT IN THE CITY, BUT I NEVER HEAR HORSE OR CARRIAGE. DO YOU WONDER HOW THIS CAN BE? BECAUSE A SOUL UNATTACHED CREATES ITS OWN SWEET SOLITUDE.

I PICK CHRYSANTHEMUMS UNDER THE HEDGE TO THE EAST, GAZE AT THE MOUNTAIN RISING TO THE SOUTH, BREATHE HIGH WESTERN AIR AT SUNSET, WATCH THE BIRDS FLY NORTH.

THESE THINGS HOLD HIDDEN TRUTHS . . . BUT WHEN I TRY TO UNCOVER THEM, WORDS ARE NOT THE WAY. [*Tao Yuan-Ming*]

• • •

THE INSTRUMENT

I SET MY STRINGED INSTRUMENT HERE ON THE ELEGANT TABLE . . . I SIT HERE ON THE EXQUISITE BENCH. EMOTIONS FLOW INTO ME, MOVE ME, AS I SIT HERE QUIETLY.

WHY SHOULD I PLAY? BREEZES WILL FIND THE INSTRUMENT . . . BREEZES WILL FLOW OVER IT AND SWEEP THE STRINGS TO SONG. [*Po Chu-i*]

A DREAM OF YOU

FOR TEN YEARS I HAVE BEEN LIVING AND YOU HAVE BEEN DEAD. EVEN WHEN I DO NOT THINK OF YOU I CANNOT FORGET. YOUR LONELY GRAVE IS A THOUSAND MILES AWAY . . . WHERE CAN I GO TO SPEAK MY SADNESS?

EVEN IF WE MET NOW, YOU WOULD NEVER RECOGNIZE ME. MY HAIR IS GOING GRAY AT THE TEMPLES, MY WRINKLED FACE ALWAYS COVERED WITH DUST OF THE ROAD.

IN A DREAM LAST NIGHT I CAME HOME. AT THE OPEN WINDOW OF OUR ROOM YOU SAT COMBING YOUR HAIR. WE STARED AT EACH OTHER WITHOUT A WORD, AND BURST INTO TEARS. . . . I CHERISH IN MEMORY THAT GLEN OF OUR HEARTBREAKING, THAT STILL MOONLIGHT NIGHT, THAT HILL OF LITTLE PINES. [*Su Shih*]

• • •

A SONG OUT THERE

A SONG OUT THERE . . . WHY, IT IS A BEGGAR SINGING! IF THIS OLD MAN WHO NEVER HAD A SILVER COIN CAN SING, WHY MUST YOU WITH RICH GOLD MEMORIES SIT HERE AND SIGH? [*Tu Fu*]

THINKING OF HER LOVER

THE FRAGRANCE IS BLOWN FROM THE LOTUS-FLOWERS. THE EMERALD LEAVES ARE WITHERED NOW AND BROWN. THE WEST WIND IS PUFFING SORROWS INTO GREEN RIPPLES ON THE RIVER. EVERYTHING IS DYING, MY YEARS ARE DYING . . . I CANNOT BEAR THE SIGHT OF DEATH.

I STARE AT THE SILKEN LINES OF RAIN, WHERE MY DREAMS ARE FLOATING IN THE LOST LANDS OF NEVERMORE. ALONE I BLOW ON MY FLUTE OF JADE, UNTIL MY BALCONY FREEZES WITH THE ICY NOTES. O ENDLESS SORROWS, ENDLESS TEARS, ENDLESS LEANINGS ON MY EMPTY BALCONY.

[*Prince Li Chin*]

• • •

AUTUMN MOON

THE JADE STAIRCASE WEEPS WITH DEW. IT WETS HER SILKEN SHOES, AS SHE CLIMBS SLOWLY TO THE PAVILION.

SHE TOO WEEPS. LETTING DOWN A CURTAIN OF CRYSTAL BEADS LIKE A TINKLING WATERFALL, SHE SITS STARING THROUGH IT AT THE AUTUMN MOON.

[*Li Po*]

LI-SI DANCING

IN THE IMPERIAL GARDEN BREEZES TOY WITH OPENING LOTUS BLOSSOMS. ON THE TERRACE, LYING ON SILK CUSHIONS SCATTERED THERE, THE KING LIES RESTING.

MORE DELICATE THAN A THIN SCARF OF MIST, BRIGHTER THAN THE EASTERN STAR, LI-SI THE BEAUTY, THE FAVORITE, DANCES FOR THE KING.

ALL TREMULOUS EYELIDS AND TREMBLING LIMBS, SHE CIRCLES AND DROPS BESIDE THE KING . . . UNDER THE ROYAL EYE, HER LIDS ARE LOWERED.

[*Li Po*]

• • •

REFLECTIONS

RAPIDLY TONIGHT MY BOAT FLOATS DOWN THE RIVER UNDER A CLOUD-DAPPLED SKY. I LOOK INTO THE WATER; IT IS AS CLEAR AS THE NIGHT. WHEN CLOUDS FLOAT PAST THE MOON, I SEE THEM FLOATING IN THE RIVER, AND FEEL I AM ROWING IN THE SKY.

I THINK OF MY LOVE . . . MIRRORED SO IN MY HEART.

[*Tu Fu*]

AT MIDNIGHT

LOOK: MOONLIGHT SHINING ON MY BED. OR IS IT THE WHITE OF FROST?

RAISING MY HEAD, I SEE THE MOON OVER MOUNTAINS. LOWERING IT, I REMEMBER ALL MY DEBTS AND ERRORS.

[*Li Po*]

• • •

AN ELEGY

LAST, BEST-LOVED DAUGHTER OF OLD HSIEH, YOU WHO FOOLISHLY RAN OFF WITH THAT PENNILESS BOY, WHO MENDED HIS CLOTHES WITH PATCHES FROM YOUR OLD CLOTHES BROUGHT FROM HOME . . . AND I TEASED YOU FOR YOUR GOLD HAIRPINS, SO WE COULD TRADE FOR WINE, AND WE DRANK IT WITH OUR DINNERS OF BERRIES AND HERBS PICKED CHEAP IN THE FIELD, COOKED OVER DRY LEAVES FROM THE FIELD . . . NOW, WHEN THEY PAY ME WELL, ALL I CAN GIVE BACK TO YOU IS TEMPLE OFFERINGS.

LONG LONG AGO WE COULD LAUGH AT DYING, BUT DEATH A MAGICIAN CLOSED YOU IN HIS HAND AND OPENED IT SUDDENLY EMPTY. I HAVE LOCKED YOUR NEEDLEWORK AWAY, I HAVE GIVEN YOUR

CLOTHES AWAY . . . MY EYES ARE NOT STRONG ENOUGH. I AM GENTLE, BECAUSE YOU WERE, TO OUR SERVING-MAIDS AND MEN. SOMETIMES WHEN I DREAM I DREAM I SHOWER YOU WITH GIFTS. ALL OF US MUST KNOW SUCH SORROW . . . TO KNOW IT BEST YOU MUST FIRST BE POOR AND HAPPY TOGETHER.

HERE I SIT ALONE, HERE I SIGH FOR BOTH OF US. HOW MANY BEADS MUST I STILL COUNT UPON MY STRING OF TIME? BETTER MEN THAN I HAVE GROWN OLD WITHOUT A SON . . . A BETTER POET SANG TO HIS DEAD WIFE WHO COULD NOT HEAR.

WE NEVER SAID THAT WE WOULD MEET AGAIN IN DEATH. I HAVE NO HOPE BEYOND THE DARKNESS. ALL I HAVE, IS TO STARE INTO THE NIGHT, SEEING AGAIN AND AGAIN THAT LITTLE WORRIED WRINKLE IN YOUR BROW.

[*Yuan Chen*]

• • •

THIS VOLUME
HAS BEEN PREPARED
PRINTED AND
PUBLISHED AT
THE OFFICE
OF THE
PETER PAUPER PRESS
MOUNT VERNON
NEW YORK